Primary Teachers LOVE These Poems

Written by **GWEN PETREMAN**

Order this book online at www.trafford.com
or email orders@trafford.com

Most Trafford titles are also available at major online book retailers.

Printed in the United States of America.

ISBN: 978-1-4907-5015-6 (sc)
       978-1-4907-5014-9 (e)

Because of the dynamic nature of the Internet, any web addresses or links contained in this book may have changed since publication and may no longer be valid. The views expressed in this work are solely those of the author and do not necessarily reflect the views of the publisher, and the publisher hereby disclaims any responsibility for them.

Any people depicted in stock imagery provided by Thinkstock are models, and such images are being used for illustrative purposes only.
Certain stock imagery © Thinkstock.

Trafford rev. 12/03/2014

 www.trafford.com

North America & international
toll-free: 1 888 232 4444 (USA & Canada)
fax: 812 355 4082

Get Ready To Listen

Sit down small,
Stand up tall,
Arms up high,
Touch the sky.

Sit down small,
Stand up tall,
Arms out wide,
Down at your side.

Sit down small,
Stand up tall,
Touch your nose,
Tap your toes.

Sit down small,
Stand up tall,
Point to the door,
Touch the floor.

Sit down small,
Stand up tall,
Slap your knees,
Wave, wave please.

Sit down small,
Stand up tall,
Tap your head,
Point to red.

Sit down small,
Clap, clap, clap,
Snap, snap, snap,
Sh—sh—sh!
Hands in lap!

Action Number Poem

One, two (clap)
Point to blue
Slap your knees
Jump, jump, please.

Three, four
Stamp the floor
Slap your knees
Jump, jump, please.

Five, six
Lift some bricks
Slap your knees
Jump, jump, please.

Seven, eight
Paint the gate
Slap your knees
Jump, jump, please.

Nine, ten
Jog to Ben
Slap your knees
Jump, jump, please
Snap, snap, snap
Clap, clap, clap
Hands in lap.

Point to Red Red Red!

Red, red, red
I love red!
Point to red, red, red
Tap your head, head, head.
Bend your knees
Wave, wave please.

Blue, blue, blue
I love blue!
Point to blue, blue, blue
Touch your shoe, shoe, shoe.
Bend your knees
Wave, wave please.

Yellow, yellow, yellow
I love yellow!
Point to yellow, yellow, yellow
Eat your Jell-O, Jell-O, Jell-O
Bend your knees
Wave, wave please.

Green, green, green
I love green!
Point to green, green, green
Eat your bean, bean, bean.
Bend your knees
Wave, wave please.

White, white, white
I love white!
Point to white, white, white
Fly your kite, kite, kite.
Bend your knees
Wave, wave please.

Black, black, black
I love black!
Point to black, black, black
Scratch your back, back, back.
Bend your knees
Wave, wave please.

Pink, pink, pink
I love pink!
Point to pink, pink, pink
Clean your sink, sink, sink.
Bend your knees
Wave, wave please.

Brown, brown, brown,
I love brown!
Point to brown, brown, brown
Time to sit down, down, down.
Clap, clap ,clap,
Hands in lap.

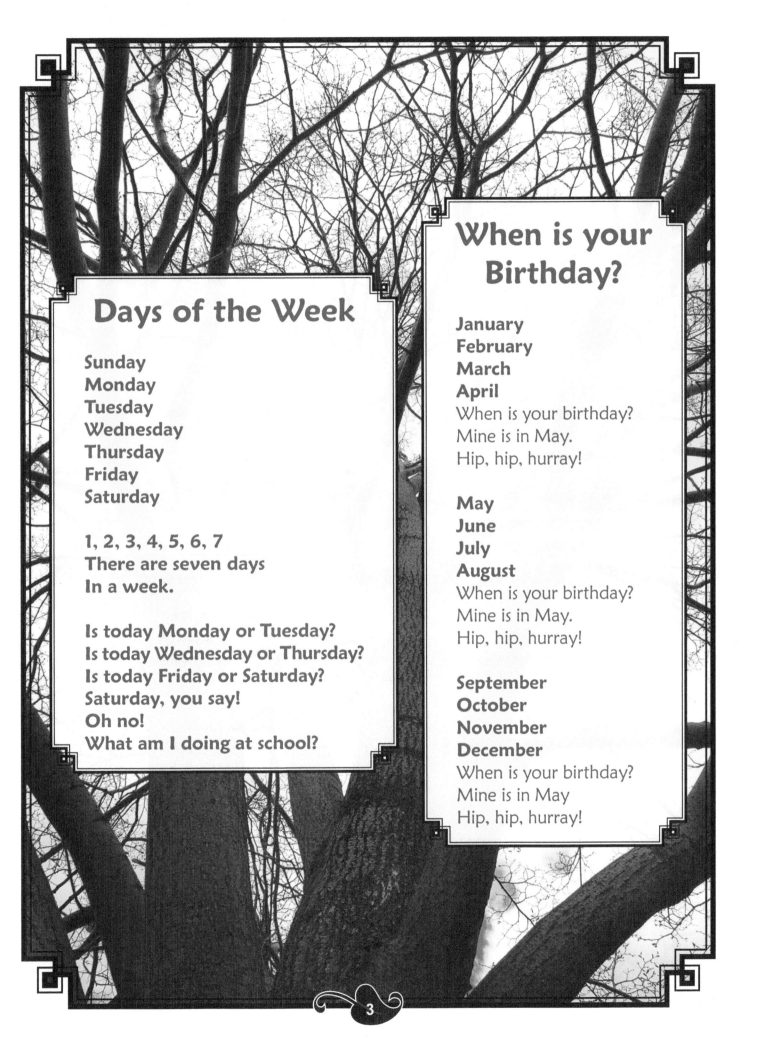

Days of the Week

Sunday
Monday
Tuesday
Wednesday
Thursday
Friday
Saturday

1, 2, 3, 4, 5, 6, 7
There are seven days
In a week.

Is today Monday or Tuesday?
Is today Wednesday or Thursday?
Is today Friday or Saturday?
Saturday, you say!
Oh no!
What am I doing at school?

When is your Birthday?

January
February
March
April
When is your birthday?
Mine is in May.
Hip, hip, hurray!

May
June
July
August
When is your birthday?
Mine is in May.
Hip, hip, hurray!

September
October
November
December
When is your birthday?
Mine is in May
Hip, hip, hurray!

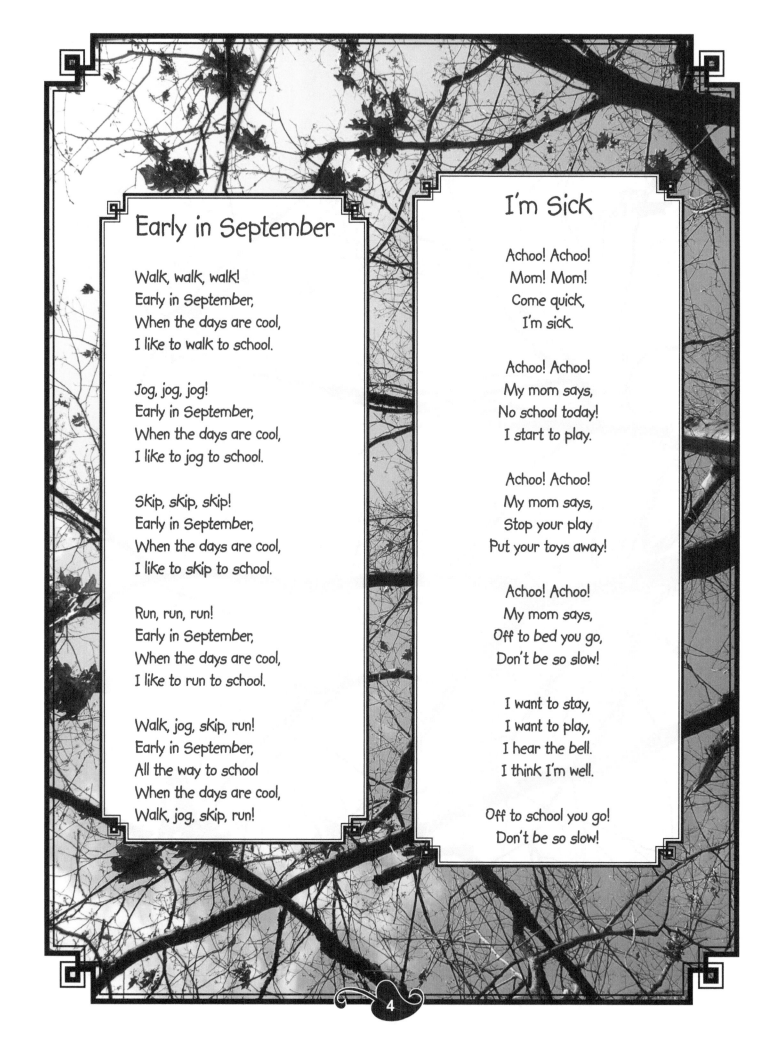

Early in September

Walk, walk, walk!
Early in September,
When the days are cool,
I like to walk to school.

Jog, jog, jog!
Early in September,
When the days are cool,
I like to jog to school.

Skip, skip, skip!
Early in September,
When the days are cool,
I like to skip to school.

Run, run, run!
Early in September,
When the days are cool,
I like to run to school.

Walk, jog, skip, run!
Early in September,
All the way to school
When the days are cool,
Walk, jog, skip, run!

I'm Sick

Achoo! Achoo!
Mom! Mom!
Come quick,
I'm sick.

Achoo! Achoo!
My mom says,
No school today!
I start to play.

Achoo! Achoo!
My mom says,
Stop your play
Put your toys away!

Achoo! Achoo!
My mom says,
Off to bed you go,
Don't be so slow!

I want to stay,
I want to play,
I hear the bell.
I think I'm well.

Off to school you go!
Don't be so slow!

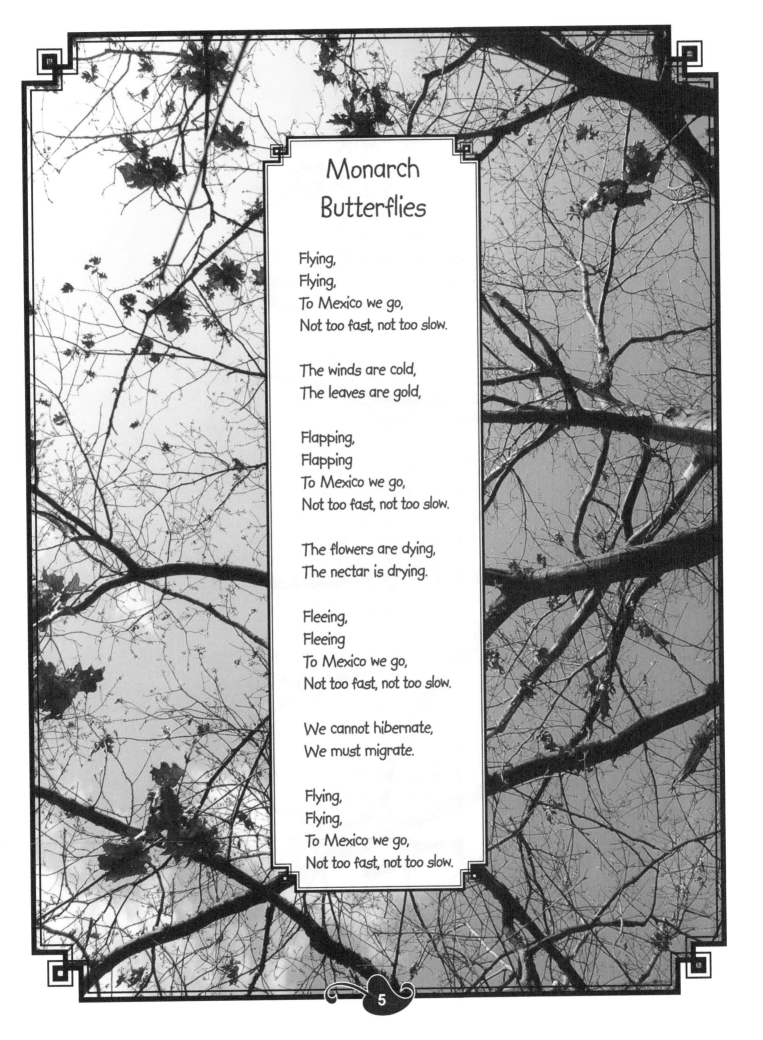

Monarch
Butterflies

Flying,
Flying,
To Mexico we go,
Not too fast, not too slow.

The winds are cold,
The leaves are gold,

Flapping,
Flapping
To Mexico we go,
Not too fast, not too slow.

The flowers are dying,
The nectar is drying.

Fleeing,
Fleeing
To Mexico we go,
Not too fast, not too slow.

We cannot hibernate,
We must migrate.

Flying,
Flying,
To Mexico we go,
Not too fast, not too slow.

Autumn Leaves

Red leaves,
Orange leaves,
Yellow and brown.

Gently, gently falling,
All over the ground.

Red leaves,
Orange leaves,
Yellow and brown.

Gently, gently dancing,
All over town.

Red leaves,
Orange leaves,
Yellow and brown.

Gently, gently floating,
Without a single sound.

Red leaves,
Orange leaves,
Yellow and brown.

Gently, gently . . .
Falling, dancing, floating,
On the ground,
In the town,
Without a sound.

Thanksgiving

Gobble, gobble, gobble!
What's that sound?
Is that a cat
Hissing at a rat?

No! No! No!
It's a turkey
It's Thanksgiving.

Gobble, gobble, gobble!
What's that sound?
Is that a hog
Snoring on a log?

No! No! No!
It's a turkey
It's Thanksgiving.

Gobble, gobble, gobble!
What's that sound?
IT'S A TURKEY!

Apples

Red apples,
Yellow apples,
Green apples,
I love apples!

Apple pie,
Apple crisp,
Crunch, crunch, crunch,
Yum! Yum! Yum!
For my lunch.

Red apples,
Yellow apples,
Green apples,
I love apples!

Apple juice,
Apple sauce,
Munch, munch, munch,
Yum! Yum! Yum!
For my lunch.

Red apples,
Yellow apples,
Green apples,
I love apples!

Fresh apples,
Ripe apples,
Bite, bite, bite,
Yuck! Yuck! Yuck!
WORMS LOVE APPLES TOO!

It's Halloween

It's Halloween!
I'M SCARED!
I'm shaking!
I have goose bumps!

Is that a ghost floating through the air?
Is that a goblin pulling at my hair?

It's Halloween!
I'M SCARED!
I'm shaking!
I have goose bumps!

Is that a rat eating my toast?
Is that a cat chasing a ghost?

It's Halloween!
I'M SCARED!
I'm shaking!
I have goose bumps!

Is that a witch baking a cricket pie?
Is that a vampire bat flying by?

It's Halloween!
I'M SCARED!
I'm shaking!
I have goose bumps!

Is that a tarantula creeping across my floor?
Is that a scary monster opening the door?

It's not a MONSTER!
It's my DAD!
I'M NOT SCARED!
I'm not shaking!
I don't have goose bumps!
BUT IT'S STILL HALLOWEEN!

Remembrance Day

It's Remembrance Day.

I wear a poppy of red,
I bow down my head.

I remember . . .
I remember . . .

The men
The women
The children.

The ones who cried,
The ones who died.

I wear a poppy of red,
I bow down my head.

I pray . . .
I pray . . .

For the soldiers,
For the peacekeepers.

It's Remembrance Day
I remember . . .
I pray . . .
For peace
Forever more.

What is Your Race?

I stare
You glare
I compare
Your face
My face
What is your race?

One mouth
One nose

Two eyes
Two ears
Two hands
Two feet

Ten fingers
Ten toes.

I stare
I compare
Your face
My face
We
all
belong
to
the
HUMAN
RACE.

Winter is Here

Spring, summer,
Fall, winter,
Winter is here,
Give a cheer,
Hip! Hip! Hurray!

Snow is falling
On the ground
In the town.

Spring, summer,
Fall, winter,
Winter is here,
Give a cheer,
Hip! Hip! Hurray!

Snow is dancing
On the breeze
Through the trees.

Spring, summer,
Fall, winter,
Winter is here
Give a cheer,
Hip! Hip! Hurray!

Snow, Snow

Snow! Snow!
Frosty feathers
Floating… Fluttering…
On my face
Looks like lace.

Snow! Snow!
Flakey flurries
Trembling…Tickling…
My ice-cold nose
Red as a rose.

Snow! Snow!
Blinding blizzard
Rushing…Racing…
Near and far
Like a racing car.

Ho! Ho! Ho!

Santa's putting on his suit,
Ho! Ho! Ho!
Oh no! He can't find his boot.
Ho! Ho! Ho!

Santa searched high and low,
Ho! Ho! Ho!
He found his boot in the snow.
Ho! Ho! Ho!

Santa jumped on his sleigh,
Ho! Ho! Ho!
Rudolph is leading the way.
Ho! Ho! Ho!

Santa put a gift under my tree,
Ho! Ho! Ho!
Hurray! The gift is for me!
Ho! Ho! Ho!

I wonder what it could be?

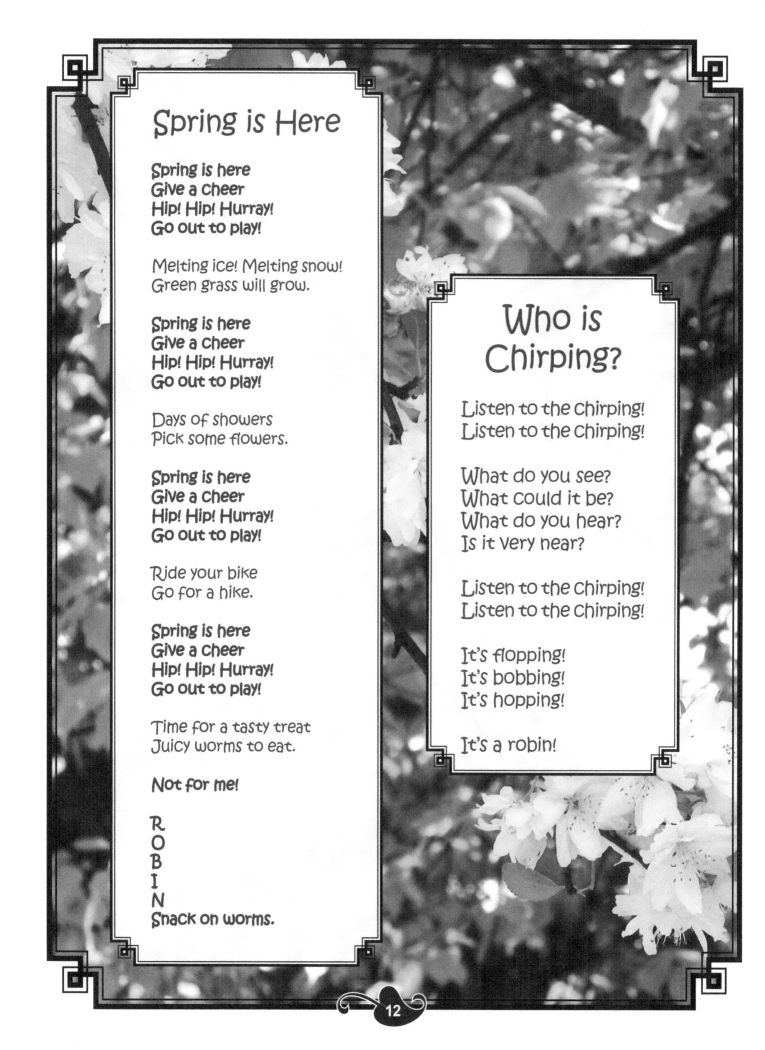

Spring is Here

Spring is here
Give a cheer
Hip! Hip! Hurray!
Go out to play!

Melting ice! Melting snow!
Green grass will grow.

Spring is here
Give a cheer
Hip! Hip! Hurray!
Go out to play!

Days of showers
Pick some flowers.

Spring is here
Give a cheer
Hip! Hip! Hurray!
Go out to play!

Ride your bike
Go for a hike.

Spring is here
Give a cheer
Hip! Hip! Hurray!
Go out to play!

Time for a tasty treat
Juicy worms to eat.

Not for me!

R
O
B
I
N
Snack on worms.

Who is Chirping?

Listen to the chirping!
Listen to the chirping!

What do you see?
What could it be?
What do you hear?
Is it very near?

Listen to the chirping!
Listen to the chirping!

It's flopping!
It's bobbing!
It's hopping!

It's a robin!

My Flower

Pull some weeds
Plant some seeds.

Roots reaching down
Way below the ground.

Stems round and tall
Leaning on the wall.

Leaves big and green
Biggest I've ever seen.

What could the flower be?
Stretching taller than me.

It's a sunflower!

I Love Trees!

Trees! Trees! Trees!
I love trees!

Hug a tree
Plant a tree
Water a tree
For you
For me
For Mother Earth

Trees! Trees! Trees!
I love trees!

The Months

January

Lots of snow,

Hear the winds blow.

It must be January,

The first month of the year.

February

Days crisp and cold,

Skiers swift and bold.

It must be February,

The second month of the year.

March

Kites flying high,

Warmer winds blowing by.

It must be March,

The third month of the year.

April

Days and days of showers,

Soon we'll see the flowers,

It must be April,

The fourth month of the year.

May

The robins have all come back,

Searching for a wormy snack.

It must be May,

The fifth month of the year.

June

Tiny seeds planted in a row,

Soon we'll see them grow.

It must be June,

The sixth month of the year.

The Months

July

Days hazy and hot,

Look for a shady spot.

It must be July,

The seventh month of the year.

August

The corn is ripe and high,

Sunflowers reach for the sky.

It must be August,

The eighth month of the year.

September

Back to school for girls and boys,

Put away your summer toys.

It must be September,

The ninth month of the year.

October

Colourful leaves fall down,

Frost starts to touch the ground.

It must be October,

The tenth month of the year.

November

A white blanket of snow,

Poppies to remember long ago.

It must be November,

The eleventh month of the year.

December

Santa, gifts, Christmas lights,

Long, freezing winter nights.

It must be December,

The twelfth month of the year.

CPSIA information can be obtained at www.ICGtesting.com
Printed in the USA
LVOW02s0453080115

421920LV00003B/5/P